Joh...G...g

I...

Mary Boone

Raintree is an imprint of Capstone Global Library Limited, a company incorporated in England and Wales having its registered office at 264 Banbury Road, Oxford, OX2 7DY – Registered company number: 6695582

www.raintree.co.uk
myorders@raintree.co.uk

Edited by Anna Butzer
Designed by Bobbie Nuytten
Picture research by Jo Miller
Production by Laura Manthe
Originated by Capstone Global Library Limited
Printed and bound in India.

ISBN 978 1 4747 5535 1 (hardcover)   ISBN 978 1 4747 5540 5 (paperback)
22 21 20 19 18   23 22 21 20 19 18
10 9 8 7 6 5 4 3 2 1   10 9 8 7 6 5 4 3 2 1

British Library Cataloguing in Publication Data
A full catalogue record for this book is available from the British Library.

Acknowledgements
We would like to thank the following for permission to reproduce photographs: Alamy: Cronicle, 19; Granger, NYC - All rights reserved., 7; Newscom: akg-images, 5, Design Pics, 17, Glasshouse Images, 9, Li Muzi Xinhua News Agency, 15, Pictures from History, 11, World History Archive, 13; Shutterstock: Everett Historical, cover (both), 1, Rainer Lesniewski, 21

Design Elements
Shutterstock: Rainer Lesniewski

Contents

CHAPTER 1

Simple beginnings

Johannes Gutenberg made big changes to how books were printed. He introduced **movable type** and the printing press to Europe. Before his inventions, making a single book could take hundreds of hours. Johannes was a **craftsman** whose press made it possible to share ideas more easily.

movable type printing type made of individual pieces that can be rearranged to make different words

craftsman worker who practises a craft that requires skill with his hands

5

Johannes was born around 1395 in Mainz, Germany. In 1411 a **political** battle in Mainz made it too dangerous to stay there. He and his family packed up their belongings. They moved to what is now Strasbourg, France. While in France, Johannes worked for a **goldsmith** who taught him how to make coins.

political relating to the things people do to gain or keep power

goldsmith person who makes gold jewellery or other items

Mainz, Germany, around
the time of Johannes' birth

CHAPTER 2

Changing books forever

Johannes began printing
with metal type in the 1430s. His
goldsmithing skills came in handy.
He already knew how to make
moulds. Now he poured **molten**
metal into them to make individual
letters. Johannes soon used these
letters to improve the way printing
presses worked.

moulds containers that are used to
give shape to something that is
poured or pressed into them

molten melted by heat into a liquid;
molten metal can be poured into moulds

Johannes (right) examining a page
printed on his press, 15th century

Johannes made his first movable type press in about 1440. Before movable type, printers used block printing. The wooden blocks had to be hand carved and could only create one message or design. With movable type, the letters could be reused and rearranged for each new page.

Other print pioneers

Johannes introduced printing to Europe, but he wasn't the first person in the world to use the process. Around 1040 a Chinese peasant called Bi Sheng used baked clay to develop a printing system. In 1377 a collection of Zen Buddhist books were created in Korea using metal movable type.

Johannes' new invention made it much easier and faster to print books. Without the movable press, every single word you read would be handwritten or carved. Before the press, very few books were **published**. Only wealthy people could afford them. Johannes helped make information available to more people.

FACT Researchers believe the first project Johannes printed with his press was a Latin textbook called *Ars Minor*.

publish make and distribute a book, magazine, newspaper or any other printed material so that people can buy it

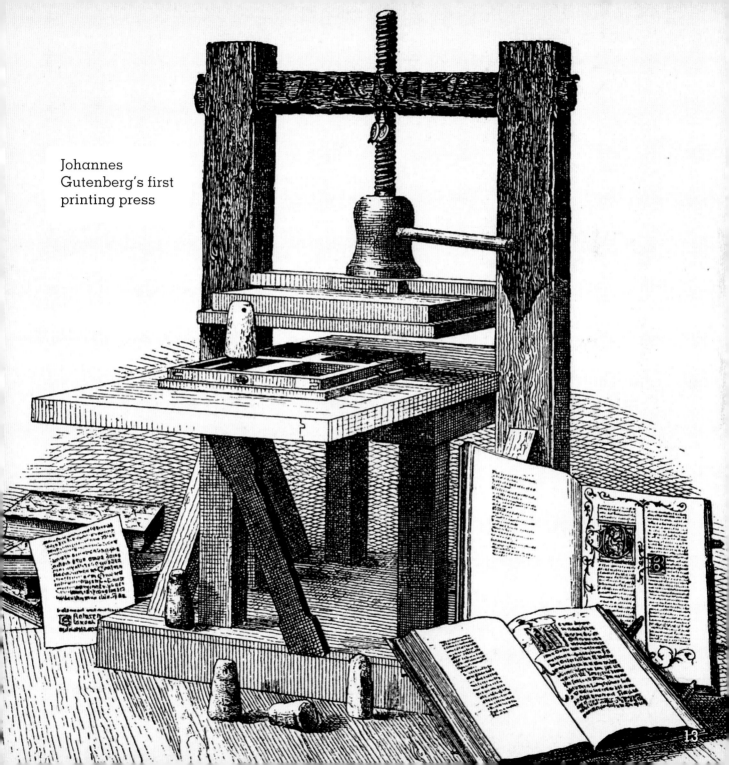

Johannes Gutenberg's first printing press

13

In 1455 Johannes began printing the 42-line Bible. It was given this name because it had 42 lines of print on each page. It later became known as the Gutenberg Bible. It was the first book **mass-produced** in Europe. Historians believe 180 copies of the Bible were made.

Book notes

Not all Gutenberg Bibles were exactly alike. Most were 1,286 pages long. In the beginning, red ink was used to print chapter headings. Printing in two colours took a lot of time. Johannes began leaving a blank space so owners could hire artists to add headings and illustrations.

mass-produced make very large amounts of something, usually by using machinery

FACT Only about 49 original Gutenberg Bibles still exist. The last one to be sold was purchased in 1987 for $5.4 million.

A Gutenberg Bible at the Morgan Library and Museum in New York City, USA

CHAPTER 3

A life filled with challenge

Johannes moved back to Germany around 1448. He borrowed money from businessman Johann Fust to build a print shop. Johannes soon owed so much money he could not pay back the loan. Fust **sued** Johannes and won. He took over most of Johannes' businesses, including the production of his Bibles.

sue take legal action against someone

Johann Fust (left), Johannes Gutenberg (centre) and a fellow print shop worker (right)

Johannes was discouraged, but he did not give up. He started another small printing business. In 1462 a battle broke out in Mainz. The fighting destroyed both Fust's and Johannes' printing businesses. Johannes stayed in Mainz, but once again found himself poor and without a job.

Destruction of a printing press in Mainz, Germany

In 1465 the **Archbishop** of Mainz gave Johannes a job within the church. It allowed him to earn a little money and continue his printing work. Historians believe he went blind in the last months of his life. Johannes died on 3 February 1468.

What's old is new again

When Johannes started making books, everything was done by hand. Even after he developed the press, pages were sewn together with a needle and thread. Technology has changed that, but some artists want to keep these old ways alive. Some universities now offer classes in book arts and printmaking.

archbishop leader in the Catholic Church in charge of a city or area

Johannes Gutenberg monument in Strasbourg, France

FACT No one knows exactly how many books have been published in modern history. However, researchers say the answer is about 130 million.

Glossary

archbishop leader in the Catholic Church in charge of a city or area

craftsman worker who practises a craft that requires skill with his hands

goldsmith person who makes gold jewellery or other items

mass-produce make very large amounts of something, usually by using machinery

molten melted by heat into a liquid; molten metal can be poured into moulds

moulds containers that are used to give shape to something that is poured or pressed into them

movable type printing type made of individual pieces that can be rearranged to make different words

political relating to the things people do to gain or keep power

publish produce and distribute a book, magazine, newspaper or any other printed material so that people can buy it

sue take legal action against someone